Joyce Jillson's™ Astrology for Cats

By Joyce Jillson
Illustrated by Ronald Lipking

BOWTIE P R E S S®

Irvine, California
A Division of BowTie, Inc.

Karla Austin, *Business Operations Manager*
Nick Clemente, *Special Consultant*
Jarelle S. Stein, *Editor*
Kendra Strey, *Assistant Editor*
Jill Dupont, *Production*
Janet Moir McCaffrey, *Book Designer*

Library of Congress Cataloging-in-Publication Data

Jillson, Joyce.
 Joyce Jillson's Astrology for cats / by Joyce Jillson ; illustrator, Ronald Lipking.
  p. cm.
 ISBN 1-931993-29-7 (softcover : alk. paper)
 1. Astrology and pets. 2. Cats--Miscellanea. I. Title.

 BF1728.3.J55 2005
 133.5--dc22

                              2004015793

BowTie Press®
A Division of BowTie, Inc.
3 Burroughs
Irvine, California 92618

Printed and bound in Singapore
10 9 8 7 6 5 4 3 2 1

to all the cats in the world, especially the cats who ate my homework, and to KHU in particular.

—joyce jillson

Joyce Jillson, internationally syndicated astrologer to the stars and major corporations, enjoyed life on a universal scale until her death, October 1, 2004.

Animals, from her three Great Danes, Jupiter, Gemini and Neptune; her many cats and in particular, her special 500-pound lion buddy, Donny, whom she led on a frail leash were Joyce's friends of choice. She believed they possessed psychic abilities enabling her to build relationships with them on a higher and more intimate level.

Joyce was not alone when she said, "Every creature has a unique chart, just as every pet has its own personality. We love each of them and cater to their strengths and frailties."

She's not alone now. We and her furry friends miss her already.

—Steve Adler

Contents

WHAT IS

CAT ASTROLOGY?

Introduction

Every cat owner realizes how unique her cat can be and treats her accordingly. Cats have individual personalities, sometimes similar to and sometimes different from their owners. Carl Jung studied astrology and believed that the stars have a profound effect on the timing of events for people and animals. He called this the "universal connection." Taking a cue from Jung, we can apply the universal connection to our felines.

Astrology focuses on the zodiac, an imaginary heavenly belt extending on each side of the apparent path of the sun, including the paths of the moon and principal planets except for Pluto. Each planet is part of a sun sign. Astrological sun signs are divided into four elements: water, air, earth, and fire. These symbols originated in biblical times, when lifestyles and harvests literally revolved around the sun.

The zodiac is divided into twelve equal sun signs named for a different constellation, each with its own symbol: **Aries** (The Ram), **Taurus** (The Bull), **Gemini** (The Twins), **Cancer** (The Crab), **Leo** (The Lion), **Virgo**

(The Virgin), **Libra** (The Scales), **Scorpio** (The Scorpion), **Sagittarius** (The Horse), **Capricorn** (The Goat), **Aquarius** (The Water Bearer), and **Pisces** (Two Fish).

The twelve categories of life—the mini-zodiac—are divided into houses or sections (similar to the zodiac's twelve signs): individuality, finances, communications, home, creativity, improving daily life, relationships, transitions, personal growth, achievement, friendship, and the inner self.

A kitty Petrology Forecast—determined by a combination of her sun sign, houses, and planet positions, considers the position of the planets, including the sun and moon, at the time of the pet's birth. Your cat's symbol tells you about her basic nature and how she will fit into your household. For example, a cat born under the royal sign of Leo is fated to rule her environment.

Cats with a water sun sign (Cancer, Scorpio, or Pisces) tend to carry instinctive and sympathetic traits. The three air sun signs (Gemini, Libra, or Aquarius) are often responsive and smart. (People often mistake Aquarius for a water sign because its symbol is the Water Bearer.) Earth sun signs (Taurus, Virgo, or Capricorn) are full of ingenuity and persistence. The flaming sun signs (Aires, Leo, or Sagittarius) are more aggressive, tireless, and friendly.

Using the age-old art of astrology, you can learn how to get in sync with your complex creature. Understanding your cat's astrology can help you better understand your furry significant other.

Determining Your Cat's Birth Date

The last time I asked a cat for his birth date, all I received was a bored stare. If you know your cat's breeder or were present when the kitten was born, then you're among the lucky few. For the rest of us, investigative work may be necessary. First, contact your cat's breeder or store or shelter where you found your kitty. If your cat's birth date was documented, you will be able to determine his sun sign and go from there. If you cannot pinpoint your cat's birthday, celebrate the day he came into your household. After all, this is the birth of your relationship, and knowing the stars' imprint on that relationship gives you more knowledge about how to love, nurture, and live with your animal partner.

Cat owners who did not note the day their cat came home should read about all twelve signs. Decide which one best describes your furry friend and determine your cat's sign based upon his personality traits.

ARIES

March 21—April 19

The Aries Cat

Your Aries cat has vivacity that matches her spring-time birthday. Born at the beginning of the zodiac, her excitement for new experiences is catching. Aries is ruled by Mars, meaning her energy is direct and forceful. Therefore, your cat is naturally curious, which might get her into a few snags. You need to keep a close eye on her adventuresome spirit. She's not one to step down from a confrontation, so you might not want to let her roam the streets for too long. Curbing her cruising time should prevent any unnecessary scratches and scuffles. Aggressive indoor play with engaging and colorful toys will help your cat use up her desire to fight.

A natural benefit of your warring cat is that you will have nary a mouse in the house. She will swiftly dispose of small intruders. She'll race to the door every time you have a visitor, trying to figure out whether the guest is a friend or foe. It's up to you to make the introductions and set the tone for your feline friend.

Dance the night away with your physically aware Aries cat. Turn up some Cat Stevens and shake a tail together. Your kitty will enjoy the music and love scratching a rug with you. Who's the better dancer between the two of you? That's a close call!

When it's time to relax in front of the television, your Aries cat will enjoy watching extreme sports. She gets an adrenaline rush from watching humans fly through the air like birds. Soap operas also get her going—she loves that all of the characters are on the verge of a dramatic clash. Excitement is the nature of an Aries cat because sound and movement stimulate her. She will let you know she's having a good time by rapidly swishing her tail.

The Aries cat will do anything she can to get your attention—especially if there are other pets in the home. Make sure you praise her positive behavior. Keep punishments to a minimum as they will just make her act out more. All she really wants is love, and if you dole it out generously, she will return to you an energized perspective.

Let your Aries cat guide you to new levels of confidence. Her extreme energy is more inspiring than tiring, and you'll find she's quite a dynamic kitty! Your cat gives new meaning to the phrase, "Work hard, play hard." Whatever she does, she does with gusto. This energy comes from the fire in her chart. A cat with this element doesn't slowly take in the sights as she strolls through the neighborhood—she'll sprint down the street.

Aries Pawcast

Symbol:
Ram, fearless
and ambitious

Ruling planet:
Mars, the planet of passion

Key personality trait:

The Aries cat is opinionated and responds in conversation both vocally and through body language.

Favorite thing about owner:
your purposeful walk, your commanding voice, and that you know what you want and go after it

Cat idol:
Jaguar;
a powerful, large, spotted wildcat that lives in South and Central America

Mantra:

"I'm one good-looking cat."

Dating style: Outgoing. She will lock on to the object of affection and pursue the romance until the other party finally gives in. This kitty is often afflicted with love at first sight, but mating for life isn't this cat's style. An Aries cat wants variety and challenge. Somehow, being spayed doesn't affect this kitty's sex drive much. The Aries kitty is always willing to fight for the cat of her dreams. The more dangerous the fight, the more this cat will love the prize.

Best feature:
confident posture

Worst feature:
killing birds

Favorite activity with owner:
playing rough

Pet peeves:

being held like a baby and listening to baby talk

Would like more: involvement in making plans, especially regarding career or home improvement

Favorite sport:
climbing shelves

Favorite entertainment:
watching birds, flies, catfights, and televised boxing

Dreams and fantasies:
The Aries cat dreams of fighting. She loves the idea of changing into a bull and challenging a matador in a Spanish arena. Her dream fight is

Favorite food: blood-rare meat

grueling, but the bull always wins! Another favorite dream of the Aries cat might be that you win the lottery and turn your backyard into a jungle where she can hunt for the family's evening meal. The Aries cat only wishes that you too enjoyed eating mice.

TAURUS

April 20—May 20

The Taurus Cat

Beings born under the sign of Taurus have a penchant for luxury and beauty, and your cat is no exception. He certainly has a flare for the finer things in life. He can tell when you've switched to a more expensive brand of cat food and he appreciates your gesture of generosity. Never a selfish kitty, he never craves all the treats just for himself— he wants all his family members to enjoy the benefits of a charmed life. Your Taurus is a cat who looks out for his kin.

Your Taurus cat is an attentive caretaker and will always keep a watchful eye on children and other pets. If he knows something is wrong, he will promptly lead you to the source of his distress. The last thing he wants to do is leave a loved one in a bind. He's sweet to new babies and isn't easily fazed by rambunctious youngsters.

The throat is the most sensitive area of your Taurus cat, so provide him with large quantities of fresh, cool water to quench his seemingly insatiable thirst. Brush his hair frequently to get rid of extra hair before it ends up in his delicate throat. He's most miserable when he has to spend the day hacking away. He will thank you for helping him take steps to avoid hairballs.

Your Taurus cat will help you turn your house into a home. His earthy, easygoing attitude is the perfect complement to a busy family. He is as loyal as cats come. If you decide to rearrange your furniture or move, your

Taurus cat won't have any trouble adapting to the changes—just as long as you don't get rid of his favorite chair! Familiar comforts and smells mean a great deal to your Taurus cat, just as the sights and sounds of his favorite people will put him at ease.

Taurus cats quickly develop a special bond with their human parents. If you want your cat to be relaxed, place him on a luxurious cashmere blanket or a silk sheet, dim the lights, and stroke him until he feels that he is the one you love the most. If you don't have time for this ritual, your Taurus cat will understand. He is a patient kitty. He knows he will get his turn even when you're rushing around the house. He can tell when to keep his distance and when to pounce into your lap and nuzzle your neck.

As an Earth sign, he will enjoy spending a great deal of time outdoors. Even if you let him out for long walks, he will usually find his way back home to you.

Taurus Pawcast

Symbol:
Bull, determined and consistent

Ruling planet:
Venus, the planet of beauty and pleasure

Key personality trait:

A Taurus cat makes a terrific parent; mothers tend to have small litters.

Favorite thing about owner: the wonderful smell of your cooking, your gentle touch, and your warm and inviting voice

Cat idol:
Lynx; a strong wildcat found in Europe, Asia, and North America

Favorite entertainment: listening to the radio and live music, especially vocals or the harmonica

Dreams and fantasies: The Taurus cat fantasizes about being a musician strolling along the streets of Spain, meowing lovely melodies that attract scores of admiring fans, both cat and human. Another dream for the Taurus cat is that he is a food critic for a cat magazine, sampling the finest cuisine from all around the world. His discerning palate influences millions of cats and owners.

Dating style: Social. The Taurus cat enjoys getting to know other cats and takes his time in doing so. This is a sensual kitty who loves to groom, nap, cuddle and sniff, and pounce and nibble on the object of his affection. Loyalty is important to the Taurus cat. He is monogamous in relationships, but if given the opportunity, he will enjoy several different mates over the years.

Best feature: distinctive meow

Worst feature: doing exactly what humans say not to do— over and over and over

Favorite activity with owner:

sleeping in the same bed

Favorite food: lamb and rice

Would like more: Nap time with owner. This kitty enjoys the quiet, the sound of your heartbeat, and the heat of your skin. Having a rest with you on a chair after a nice meal reminds a Taurus kitty how grateful he is for being able to share all of the sights, sounds, smells, and tastes of your world. The Taurus cat would also like to hear live music once in a while, even if it's bad.

Favorite sport:
pacing

Pet peeves:

yelling in the house, dirty laundry

Mantra:

"I attract the best that life has to offer, especially in the food department."

Gemini

♊

May 21 — June 21

The Gemini Cat

G emini cats are born at the time of year when things start to heat up. Their air element gives them nimble bodies and quick minds. Gemini kitties are complex thinkers who will tell you about their feelings any chance they get. Your Gemini cat rarely has a daily agenda, but you can be sure that any of her activities will be exciting—whether strolling through the park or basking in the sun! If there were ever a chatty kitty, a Gemini cat is she! She will even try to copy the inflection in your voice. She's quite attentive and knows exactly what you're talking about even if she doesn't understand your words. But be careful what you tell your Gemini kitty—when it comes to secrets, the cat's out of the bag! Her powers of deduction verge on psychic levels. She can tell you're going on a trip even before you take her for a visit to the cat hotel. Let her in on whatever you're planning—she'll find out eventually anyway, so don't bother keeping secrets.

Who's that dancing around with your feather duster? It must be your Gemini cat! For all of her serious communication skills, she's actually sort of a goofball. Her zany sense of play makes for endless hours of entertainment for everyone. Make sure to have a camera around every time you give her a new toy or take her to an unfamiliar place. You'll never find a more curious cat!

A Gemini cat's preternatural sense of people will be an asset to you when choosing new friends. She's especially handy as an affection barometer for potential love matches. If your Gemini cat takes a liking to a guy or gal right away, you know you've got a good catch. And if she starts talking and purring, you know your date is a keeper!

Invite plenty of people and other cats over to play with your furry friend. Your Gemini cat loves to socialize and enjoys new people and places. She is nearly always up for a good time. This social trait makes a cruise her ideal vacation—there are people to chat with and plenty of scheduled stops for bird-watching and fishing.

A Gemini cat retains her childish qualities well into her golden years. She will love all of her old games even though she might not be as quick on her paws. The benefit to you is a constant infusion of youthful vitality.

Gemini Pawcast

Symbol:
Twins, intelligent and versatile

Ruling planet:
Mercury, the planet of communication and day-to-day activities

Key personality trait:

Your Gemini cat's spontaneity and verve will energize you on the grayest of mornings. (If you like to sleep in, install a cat door and leave extra food for her so she will be occupied while you snooze.)

Pet peeves: people lying about the house, stacks of unread newspapers, and inactivity

Cat idol:
Leopard; a spotted wildcat

Dreams and fantasies:

The Gemini cat imagines that she is a student, roaming the campus of an Ivy League university, cavorting with fellow cats and humans as they discuss politics and art. Oh, how impressed these school chums are with Gemini's witty insights and biting comebacks. The Gemini also often dreams she is a comedian on late-night television.

Favorite sport:
leaping from
counter to tabletop

Dating style: Flirtatious. This enchanting creature is a quick study and can be quite a seducer of cats, not to mention other species who happen to develop a forbidden crush on her. Many would like her to settle down into a comfortable domestic groove, but you'll find that your Gemini won't be caught in a monogamous relationship. However, when the romance is gone, a Gemini remains a wonderful friend and companion.

Favorite activity with owner: reading

Favorite entertainment: watching film adaptations of classic novels, watching tennis, and listening to dinner table discussions

Favorite thing about owner: your laugh when you're on the phone with friends, the way you've decorated the house, and your complex mind

Best feature:
agile paws that
solve logistical
problems like
opening doors or
breaking into sealed
food packages

Worst feature:
knocking things
off of shelves

Favorite food:
chicken

Would like more:
Exercise. Your Gemini
cat wants you to chase
her around the house,
dangle a string for her
to bat around, and allow
more outdoor time. If
you let her climb a tree
and tease some birds,
that would be terrific!
Your Gemini would also
like you to read to her
more often.

Mantra:

"I think, therefore I get tuna."

69

Cancer

June 22—July 22

The Cancer Cat

The Cancer cat's attachment to you and to his environment comes from his deeply emotional nature. Though moodiness can get the better of him, he knows how to calm himself down. This cat will quickly stake out his favorite places in the house and take a great deal of comfort in knowing that he has loving companions and a roof over his head. The Cancer cat desires security and wants to know that whoever is around will stay put. He is sensitive to relationship difficulties and will do his best to see that you and yours are happy. If there's trouble brewing, reassure your cat that you love and need him and that everything will work out for the best.

Your kitty has his special way of showing he loves you that tends to involve presenting you with small tokens of his affection, such as mice or lizards. While it may be troubling to find such a treasure on your doorstep, your cat is honoring you with his bounty. He cares about you enough to give up some of his favorite treats. Be sure not to dispose of these prizes until he's not looking. Otherwise, he might be miffed.

At his best, your Cancer cat is whimsical and silly. At his worst, he'll be broody. He keenly picks up on surrounding emotional currents. For example, you'll find he'll want to party all night with you and your friends, but he'll be there for you when you need someone to cuddle. His sign is ruled by the moon,

so he possesses its changeable nature. His emotional ups and downs are full of benefits. When he's feeling loving, he will shower you with little licks and meow for more snuggling; when he's upset, take steps to increase good vibes to combat surrounding negative energy.

Your Cancer cat is a purring prognosticator with a knack for sensing oncoming earthquakes and other natural disasters. He may even be able detect health problems in family members before there are any symptoms. Closely watch to whom your cat gravitates. This person may need your extra attention. This cat is so attuned to slight changes that he may be able to tell when you and your partner are expecting a baby—maybe even before you know!

This cat is one of few who don't mind being near the water. He probably won't go for a dip, but he enjoys lounging poolside or frolicking along the beach. His favorite way to celebrate his birthday is spending a quiet night at home with you.

Cancer Pawcast

Symbol:
Crab, a hard shell, but sensitive underside

Ruling planet:
moon, magnetically influential

Key personality trait:

Your Cancer cat might have a hard time sticking to household rules because he has a different demeanor every day. You can change his mood by modeling the behavior you would like him to have.

Cat idol:
Siberian tiger, the largest member of the cat family

Favorite sport:
stealing fish from the tank

Would like more:
Running water. Cancer cats find the shower enthralling— it's not that he wants to go in, but the sound of little drops hitting the ceramic is

Favorite thing about owner:
your singing in the shower, your smell, and your dependability

magical and calming. Also, the Cancer cat likes to be groomed because, believe it or not, he hates leaving fur on the furniture. If your Cancer cat had money, he would hire a housekeeper.

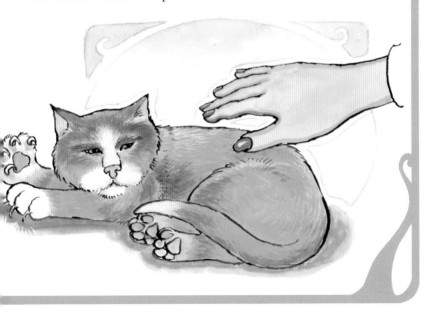

Dating style: Romantic. This kitty wants it all—an attractive catmate from a good family whose day-to-day habits are compatible with his own. Some cats jump into a love affair willy-nilly, but the Cancer cat wants to make sure that the object of his affection is a keeper before he commits to a relationship. Single Cancer cats are very attractive and usually have plenty of interested suitors sniffing at the front door.

Favorite entertainment: watching you cook and watching soap operas and home and garden television shows

Favorite food: seafood medley

Pet peeves: being misunderstood, humans hogging the bed, noisy neighbors, and the sound of a car engine

Best feature: sensitive, shimmering eyes	**Favorite activity with owner:** kicking back on the couch at the end of the day
Worst feature: overeating	**Dreams and fantasies:** The Cancer cat fantasizes about being a pirate at sea, eating all of the mice and rats on the ship, and enjoying a nice piece of

fish. A recurring dream is that he is running along a sandy shore at night, lit only by the glistening moon as it reflects in the ocean.

Mantra:

"I feel like having a snack."

Leo

July 23—August 22

The Leo Cat

T he Leo cat is a queen of the jungle trapped in a cute and cuddly little body. Her body language screams out, "I am cat. Hear me roar!" If you're not listening, this clever kitty will figure out a way to get your attention. Ruled by the sun, a Leo cat wants to be the brilliant center of your universe. She loves to put on a show for whoever is watching. Just wait until you have a group of friends over. Your cat will be the life of the party! Her desire to be noticed comes straight from the heart—she's doing all of her meowing and strutting to make sure she gets a lot of love. To her, there's no bad time to rub up against you or ask you for a treat—what else could you be doing that's more important than playing with her? She will give you endless affection in return. When this sunny cat shines, she shines brightly! If you leave her home alone for long periods of time, her spark for you might wane. She might even search around the neighborhood for new human friends who will play with her during the day.

Your reward for caring for your cat is her loyalty. She will hiss at intruders, human or animal, showing them who's in charge. Don't be surprised if your little cat is ready to take on the biggest of dogs if it means protecting you.

Leo spends an inordinate amount of time grooming because her appearance is important to her. There will be

no struggle if you brush her hair or wipe her eyes. Present your kitty with a new collar and watch her strut around the house.

When there's more than one pet in the house, a Leo cat wants to reign over all of them. She'll ensure even the meekest hamster knows who's in charge of the manor. If anyone challenges her control, she'll react with force, clawing and scratching her way to the top. Because of her leonine power, other cats naturally respect her dominion.

Your Leo cat understands the natural order of your family and won't pose a threat to children. She knows how important they are to you and treats them with respect. For all of her hustle-bustle energy, a Leo cat is a great sleeper. She adores stretching out in the afternoon sun. A warm cat makes the perfect reading companion, and she can't think of a better spot than resting on your lap.

Symbol:
Lion, proud and powerful

Leo Pawcast

Ruling planet:
sun, the star we revolve around

Key personality trait:

If you praise your Leo kitty with even the smallest gesture for good behavior, she will do it again and again.

Would like more: Attention. Scratches on the back and under the chin are always nice. Toys that show you were thinking about your Leo kitty while shopping are also greatly appreciated because Leo likes to see that you care even when you are away.

Cat idol:
MGM Lion

Favorite food: sushi

Dreams and fantasies: The Leo cat has movie star dreams in which she is on the big screen, earning the recognition of an adoring public. In these dreams, Leo is wearing sunglasses and a hat with a brim so as not to be recognized in public. She also dreams of a cat-family reunion in which all of the many kitty parents, children, sisters, brothers, uncles, aunts, and cousins could get together for a barbecue.

Dating style:

Self-absorbed. A Leo's love life is much like a kitty soap opera—fraught with melodramatic plot twists. Leo is the sign of family and the Leo cat tends to have large litters. Owners beware!

Best feature:
regal way
of sitting

Worst feature:
being careless
about using
the litterbox

Favorite entertainment:
watching movies (the more dramatic, the better), chasing things that slither, and pouncing on things that scurry

Favorite sport:
looking in the mirror

Pet peeves:
bad human breath, the smell of strong cleaning products, not being included in family entertainment, and stale water

Favorite thing about owner:
your strength and the smell of your hair

Mantra:
"Pay attention to me, people!"

Favorite activity with owner:
getting ready in the morning

August 23 — September 22

The Virgo Cat

A more perfect companion would be hard to find. Actually, perfectionism is one of the Virgo cat's most prevalent traits. Your Virgo cat believes that it is possible to be flawless, so he tries very hard to be the best cat he possibly can. He is clean, dignified, and lovely. However, the Virgo kitty holds everyone, including you, to an impossibly high standard. If you are ever late with his dinner or stingy with the catnip, you are sure to get an earful of catty remarks.

The Virgo cat is tidy. Nothing drives him crazier than a dirty litter box or a water bowl that hasn't been changed for days. When your Virgo kitty narrows his eyes in disdain and looks away from your gaze, you can be sure it's not a just a moment of odd cat behavior. It's an intentional message to make you consider your substandard behavior. Your Virgo kitty is confident that you understand him, so you may as well begin to accept the messages your cat sends.

Born under the communication planet (Mercury), Virgo understands every word you say, so keep it respectful, and more importantly, interesting. The frustrating part for your Virgo kitty is that you don't understand "Meowanese." As long as your Virgo kitty can see that you are trying to understand him, he will try to communicate with you more clearly.

Virgo is a working cat and mice won't last long in his territory. This cat considers mousing a duty, but also a practical hunger solution. The Virgo cat doesn't like to play with food, as that is seen as both cruel and a waste of time—and the Virgo cat hates waste of any kind!

Your Virgo cat is a rare feline who enjoys going to the groomer. In fact, it's the highlight of his day! Being fluffed and clipped gives him a rush of self-esteem. He doesn't think going to the vet is so bad either because he takes a great interest in his health. He prefers holistic treatment and will follow all instructions that promise to lead to better health, fitness, and beauty. A Virgo often has a long life because of his natural healing power.

If you're a person who travels without your cat, be sure you use the same kennel or cat-sitting service every time, because getting out of the groove is hard on this feline's psyche.

Your Virgo cat will inspire you to improve and will give you love in the same way that a motivational coach, a stern parent, or a wise-cracking friend might. Virgo wants to be "real" with you and he appreciates when you are the same.

Virgo Pawcast

Symbol:
The Virgin, pure and modest

Ruling planet:
Mercury, the planet of communication and day-to-day events

Key personality trait:

Your Virgo cat needs a routine, and if you stick with one, he will be content.

Cat idol:
Abyssinian cat; an ancient domestic breed with very short hair

Dreams and fantasies: Your Virgo cat dreams of being in the Amazon and stalking prey under the cover of thick, tall trees. He fantasizes about having monkey and parrot friends and enjoying activities such as chasing butterflies and hiding in thick patches of grass. Virgo also has fantasies about living on a farm.

Favorite sport:

grooming

Favorite thing about owner:
the smell of your soap, the way you do certain things at certain times each day, your kindness

Dating style: Discriminating. This cat would rather be single for a lifetime than frolic with a cat who has questionable morals or substandard breeding. He detests the cat nightlife and wouldn't be caught dead in the alley with just any old cat who happens to be in heat. However, once your Virgo cat has decided that a certain cat-prospect is up to par, he will fall head over heels in love. His love is constant and unconditional. A Virgo prefers to mate for life.

Best feature: being well-groomed

Worst feature: spitting up hairballs in inconvenient locations

Pet peeves:

untidiness—especially in the kitchen, snoring, when people drop by on the spur of the moment, eating out of the same dish as another cat

Favorite food:
tender, young
grass sprouts

Favorite entertainment:
watching
gardeners and
hummingbirds
and discovering
that a less discerning cat has made
a silly mistake with his choice of
mate

Would like more: Cleaning
and organizing from you. The
Virgo cat feels that the more
organized you are, the more
time you will have for the
truly important things in life,
such as cleaning and caring for and petting and playing
with him. Your Virgo kitty would enjoy one of those big
cat apartments with the adjoining towers and the thick
scratching post.

**Favorite activity
with owner:**
grooming

Mantra:

"I'm improving every day."

Libra

September 23—October 23

The Libra Cat

Ruled by Venus, your Libra cat holds dear the values of beauty and love. Always meticulous about grooming, she is careful to drink enough water and eat enough nutritious food to maintain a stunningly gorgeous, shiny coat and glistening eyes. The Libra cat, being an air sign, not only views humans as trusted companions but also admires humans for their intellectual capacity. This cat has a high IQ, though she feels no need to show off to you.

If you're a friend of a Libra cat, you probably noticed that she has trouble making decisions. Jump on the counter or stay on the ground? It's comical to watch a Libra cat get ready to leap and then change her mind.

One decision a Libra kitty easily makes is showering her owner with affection and unconditional love. When you come home from work, know that your Libra cat has been watching for you through the window and is ready to purr and rub up against you, affirming that you are the most important thing in her world and that you have been missed. Considering that most cats hide their feelings in favor of appearing aloof, it's quite a testament to the Libra cat's nature that she would defy the natural characteristics of her species in order to make you feel important.

It is common for a Libra cat to be on the thin side due to a high metabolism, a delicate stomach, and a desire to

look like a model. The way she sees things, a little vanity never hurt any feline! In fact, if makeup for cats existed, your Libra would wear mascara on her whiskers and dye her telltale gray hairs. A typical pampered pet, she'd certainly appreciate a shiny, new collar, maybe studded in sparkling diamonds or something similar.

Your Libra enjoys art and music. You might catch her studying a painting on your wall for hours or sitting next to the CD player when her favorite song comes on. Libra's favorite song changes with the seasons, as this kitty never likes to be behind the times, and wants everyone to think of her as hip, cool, and happening.

A Libra prefers to be in a single-cat family, but not because she doesn't enjoy the company of other animals. Rather, she wants to know you well and support you emotionally without having to compete for your time.

Though your Libra cat is extremely respectful of your furniture, carpet, and clothing, it is mostly because she considers them hers! This is especially true of your bed, which she will hog mercilessly, taking the center position in order to get as close to you as possible. Then, after much settling in, she will likely refuse to fall asleep. That's because Libra never tires of being near you.

Symbol:
Scales, for balance and justice

Libra Pawcast

Ruling planet:
Venus, the planet of pleasure and beauty

Key personality trait:

Your Libra cat longs for companionship and views her owner as a life partner

Cat idol:
Serval, an African wildcat with long, graceful legs

Would like more: Creativity in the household, such as art projects. The Libra cat loves vivid colors and would enjoy painting. She also would like you to throw more parties, big and small, and though Libra understands that she is not allowed on the dinner table during such events, she would like an honored place in the living room during the after-dinner conversation.

Favorite food: chopped beef

Pet peeves: being left alone, having a limited social life due to the inability to open the front door, too much quiet

Dating style: Needy. The quest to find the perfect cat is often superseded by the need to be part of a couple, so the Libra cat often ends up with whichever feline happens to be available. Not that this kitty is desperate, it's just that Libra's easygoing style and natural charm and good looks create a total package that has universal appeal. If there are no other cats around, your Libra cat will think of her human companions as loving partners; over time, the bond will become so satisfying that she will have no desire to see other cats.

Favorite entertainment: Mozart, watching a child's birthday party from afar, and rolling around with another cat

Favorite sport: running from one family member to the next

Favorite thing about owner: your strong arms, gentle touch, intelligent commentary on everyday things, and the way you talk to the television

Dreams and fantasies: The Libra cat dreams of lavish parties filled with cats enjoying the finest cuisine and drinking exotic milks. She also imagines being a great diplomat, a sensible and respected creature who can make the leaders of different countries connect for a meeting of the minds. And what would be their common ground? Their mutual love of cats, of course!

Favorite activity with owner: Paperwork. Libra loves to get mixed up in your papers and sit on your books while you're trying to read. The mental zone you are in while completing paperwork is very stimulating for Libra.

Best feature:
nose

Worst feature:
jumping onto your lap when you're trying to do something

Mantra:

"I'm balanced, graceful, and ready for whatever life throws my way."

♏

October 23—November 21

The Scorpio Cat

The Scorpio cat is intense, sophisticated, prone to jealousy, wildly affectionate, and driven to be the love of your life. If you've owned several cats over the years, Scorpio is the one you just don't get over. Because this kitty lives life to the fullest, the memories he creates are vivid and indelible. You can be sure that Scorpio kitty thinks of you the same way. Whereas many cats dream of fame, fortune, food, and other cats, Scorpio dreams mostly of you.

That's not to say that Scorpio doesn't play the same games that other cats do. He'll turn his back on you when he feels spurned and walk away while you're talking to him. His objective is to create drama, intrigue, and mystery. Stray cats who come to you from the streets or a shelter are often Scorpios. This circumstance often occurs out of an overwhelming need for "free love." In spite of his loyalty to you, your Scorpio cat is known to run off, often by following the cry of a female cat in heat. Sometimes, he'll lose his way during these exploits because, even though he's extremely passionate, this kitty has no conscience (and a bad sense of direction to boot). If you do not intend your Scorpio cat to breed, then it's best not to take any chances and, therefore, have him neutered. However, if you intend to breed your cat, Scorpio cats produce beautiful litters. They are born under the sign of inheritance and legacies, and they will hand down their best traits to their kittens.

One of Scorpio's favorite hobbies is surprising you. He'll

 hide in cupboards, drawers, and closets. After you haven't seen him for a while, you may think he has somehow escaped, but don't be too quick to put up Lost Cat signs. Your Scorpio kitty likely will

saunter down the hall before long. Where has he been? You may never know. Scorpio is secretive and needs his space to remain private.

Scorpio's digestive track is more delicate than others'. He does well when fed high-quality, carbon-free food. Making sure that your Scorpio cat is always drinking plenty of clean water will help him maintain a healthy urinary tract. If he's home alone for long stints, you may find he knocks things off shelves or shreds the sides of the couch. To prevent this kind of trouble, try adding another cat to your family. The more there is to do and think about, the less time your Scorpio cat will have to devote to his "home improvement" projects. If you've got a swimming pool, this cat is in heaven. He loves to hang out by the water and watch the swimming activities of humans, birds, bugs, and even dogs.

What your cat loves most is playing with you. Getting all wound up could include some feisty scratching with the front and back paws or love bites to wake you up. He's pretty good about pulling in his claws during your games, but passion occasionally overtakes him, so encourage kids not to test your Scorpio feline.

Scorpio Pawcast

Symbol:
Scorpion, mysterious and intense

Ruling planet:
Pluto, planet of regeneration and secrets

Key personality trait:

Your Scorpio cat wants you to wonder what he's thinking and to scramble for ways to please him. Believe it or not, this is the way he is thinking about you.

Cat idol:
Bengal tiger, a huge, striped wild cat

Favorite thing about owner:
that you don't put on airs, the music you listen to, and the way you always know what's hip

Would like more: Music. Every once in a while your Scorpio cat enjoys listening to a variety of music, combined with a peaceful ambiance set by candlelight and incense. He would also like you to share your dreams with him and confide in him more often. Also, he wouldn't mind an occasional massage.

Favorite sport:

chasing the new cat in town

Favorite entertainment: watching nature shows about mating habits, hanging out by the pool, and sneaking around at night

Dating style: Seductive. Your Scorpio cat understands the selflessness it takes to be wickedly attractive; he understands what his object of affection wants and how to address those desires. Scorpio is definitely not a monogamous cat, even if there are kittens involved. Every cat in the neighborhood knows where the Scorpio lives. Scorpio's kittens can be the target of vicious gossip, which he is secretly proud of and subscribes to the theory that, "All publicity is good publicity."

Best feature: slinky walk

Worst feature: loud meowing in the middle of the night

Favorite activity with owner: whispered conversations—he loves to hear a secret

Favorite food:
salmon

Pet peeves:
uptight and prudish attitudes, people who won't give him table scraps, and being kept indoors all the time

Dreams and fantasies:
Scorpio cats have risqué fantasies involving multiple cats in a convertible, a series of jungle affairs with different breeds of cats, and partying with bunnies at the Playboy mansion. Scorpio also dreams of hanging out with you at a nightclub and cruising for hot cats.

Mantra:
"I'm watching you."

The Sagittarius Cat

W ith a ruling planet like Jupiter, the Sagittarius cat is used to landing in the right place at the right time—which is exactly where she was when you came along! This sign loves to roam and explore, which explains why many Sagittarius cats are strays. A Sagittarian may try out several owners before she finds the right one. The perfect owner is the one who will afford her the freedom and independence that she holds so dear. You can never really *own* a Sagittarius cat, but you can share a home with one and, over time, earn her devotion.

Normally, cats don't travel well, but the Sagittarius cat is an exception. She doesn't mind the car, boat, or airplane. Just be sure you've got the right kind of pet carrier and never let your Sagittarius roam around in a vehicle, especially if you—the driver—are alone in the car. This cat is fearless and could interfere with driving or make a fast break out a window or open door just for the sake of sheer thrill and adventure.

Sagittarius is not an ideal indoor cat. She howls and hisses and paces as she darts under your feet at the sight of an open door. Watch the windows, too, as she can slide open screens to sneak out to the roof. She requires twice as much outdoor time as other cats and allowing this will

give her a longer life. Just be sure that she has her tags on at all times. Sagittarius is quite active, so her long fur quickly gets matted and dirty. Too bad Sagittarius doesn't like being groomed. Luckily, she'll tolerate it, especially if you change groomers every once in a while. Seeing new people puts this cat on her best behavior.

A Sagittarius cats loves an expedition and can often convince other cats that she knows cool spots to check out. If you ever see a group of strutting alley kitties, Sagittarius is probably the leader. The Sagittarius cat hates confrontation, so spraying wars between competing cats can occur.

The Sagittarius cat has a delightful talent of pointing out the little things—like the way she chases your shoelaces when you're tying them or how she sees the hummingbird out the window. The unique way she responds to everyday happenings will give you a new perspective as well. The Sagittarius cat would love you to know that the closer you look at normal things, the less normal they appear.

Sagittarius Pawcast

Symbol:
Archer, directed with high aims

Ruling planet:
Jupiter, planet of luck and abundance

Key personality trait:

This cat can be a bad influence; if you have other cats in the family, keep a close eye on behavioral trends.

Favorite thing about owner: your accent (even if you don't think you have one, your cat thinks you do), the fact that you can drive a car, your worldliness, and your optimism

Cat idol:
Snow leopard; a rare white leopard from Asia

Would like more: Traveling. Your Sagittarius cat would love a roomy cat carrier and an invitation to go wherever you go. She would also like more scheduling variety—sometimes it's fun not to know who is coming over or when dinner will be served. Sagittarius also wouldn't mind a few more pets in the household, especially something exotic or unusual like a hermit crab.

Dating style: Choosy. She prefers dating outside her breed, as exotic cats intrigue her. The Sagittarius cat would like to live in different parts of the world just to see the cultural differences in the global dating scene. This cat is prone to getting in over her head and has often been scratched or bitten by the jealous mate of one of her conquests.

Favorite sport:
sneaking out

Pet peeves:
dirty windows; not enough sitting space near the window; and anything boring, normal, or routine

Favorite entertainment:
climbing trees, watching the world from a balcony, watching the Travel Channel, and reading *National Geographic*

Favorite food:
anything imported

Dreams and fantasies:
The Sagittarius cat dreams of being an international traveler who accompanies you to different homes—spending summer in Tuscany, winter in Barbados, spring in California, and fall in Vermont. This schedule, of course, would change every year. The Sagittarius cat also fantasizes about being the first cat to walk on the moon or to explore Mars. She's convinced that humans will find feline life on Mars.

Best feature:
powerful back legs

Worst feature:
getting into trouble from her sense of sheer curiosity

Favorite activity with owner:
exploring the yard

Mantra:

"Sooner or later, I'm going to get out."

CAPRICORN

♑

December 22—January 19

The Capricorn Cat

The winter solstice is marked by the sun's passing into the sign of Capricorn, and this event has been considered by both ancient and modern scholars alike to be a magical window. Indeed, your Capricorn kitty is endowed with the impressive talents that the Capricorn sun sign offers. He is an old soul who commands respect, affinity, and admiration from all creatures in your household. Even those with seniority obey this cat's demands.

This cat is big-hearted, but he can be quite territorial. He does not share food and water with other cats, yet your Capricorn feels that you should share your food with him. He has a large ego and can be somewhat like a godfather who will fiercely protect his own while expecting a kickback of some sort in the end. This cat lives by complicated rules and rituals. Even though you may not understand his ways, you're better off accepting them.

Capricorn adores tradition and will want to be included in all family celebrations. He may keep to himself when company comes over, but he will make an appearance, much like a celebrity does when he's got several parties to attend in one night. Your Capricorn kitty will work the room, paying his respects to the critical guests, and making sure everyone gets a glimpse of his perfection.

The Capricorn cat enjoys a structured household and thinks it's his duty to account for the domestic timetable. He will wake up

just before you get home and keep track of what time you go to sleep. Some Capricorn cats are like alarm clocks, demanding food at the same hour each morning and telling everyone to get up and get moving.

The Capricorn cat is a wonderful pet for senior citizens because he will be attentive and aware, and won't dart under feet or constantly try to escape. The Capricorn cat is dignified and above causing chaos, confusion, or too much noise.

Though he hates the vet more than any other sign, Capricorn rarely has a need to go, as this cat has a hearty constitution and is generally long-lived. Capricorn is known for a wild libido, even into old age, and breeders of a Capricorn cat certainly will get more than they bargained for. Capricorn seems to always be involved in a love triangle, and the drama of pursuing new relationships is his hobby. His zest for life is perhaps his secret to longevity.

Capricorn Pawcast

Symbol:
Goat, leaping
past obstacles
to the top

Ruling planet:
Saturn, the planet of life lessons
and discipline

Key personality trait:

The Capricorn cat
adores tradition
and will want to be
in on all family
celebrations.

Cat idol:
Cougar,
a mountain lion
with a long tail

Favorite thing about owner: the way you
dress up, your thoughtfulness, the way you take
precautions such as leaving out extra food in his
dish if you think you'll be at the office late, and
your confident grip

Would like more: Work discussions. This cat would also like a bigger presence in your life outside the home, perhaps some photographs of him hung at the office, and of course you should carry around wallet-sized pictures to show everyone you meet. Your Capricorn cat cares about his reputation and would like you to circulate some good public relations on his behalf.

Favorite sport: climbing to the top of the bookshelf

Dating style: Practical. He likes to find a mate early in life and settle down so that he can get on to more important things like eating well and demonstrating his abilities to the fullest. The Capricorn cat is looking for a mate with good genes, excellent health, strong teeth, and a disciplined lifestyle. Often, Capricorn catmates will have several litters and will pair up for the long term—they prefer to think of each other as partners to grow old with.

Best feature:
shape of his head

Worst feature:
giving unwarranted, condescending looks

Pet peeves:

stupid jokes, people who state the obvious, smelly shoes and socks left out on the floor, and birds

Favorite food:
liverwurst

Favorite entertainment: participating in family reunions and watching you make business calls and type on a keyboard

Dreams and fantasies:

The Capricorn cat is a realist, and, therefore, prefers having goals to fantasies. An example of a goal is to bring home a certain number of dead things for the whole family to enjoy. (The Capricorn cat cannot understand why everyone runs away screaming at such gifts.) Other goals are to get enough exercise to keep a fit figure.

Favorite activity with owner:

strategizing how you're going to get ahead at work–he considers himself your silent, at-home business partner

Mantra:

"All right people, get to work!"

AQUARIUS

January 20—February 18

The Aquarius Cat

T he whimsical Aquarius cat is an air sign ranging in temperament from a cool refreshing breeze to a full-force tornado. This cat has the potential to turn your whole house upside down, but she is so charming that you'll overlook the chaos she creates. The Aquarius cat is accepting of everyone, which is why she makes friends easily. You, too, will make friends through your Aquarius cat because this creature attracts visitors to pet and admire her, which she adores. This is definitely not a shy feline who hides under the bed when company comes over; rather, she is the curious socialite who eagerly wants to catch up with friends.

Aquarius cats are athletic and capable of great speed. If yours is an indoor cat, watch out. She can bolt through the front door like lightning if given the chance. Be mindful of this ability when answering a knock at the door. Disgruntled Aquarius cat owners also have complained that their furry friend used the drapes as a climbing gym or the couch as a running track. To avoid damage, play with your Aquarius cat to ensure adequate exercise.

Daydreaming is a favorite pastime for your Aquarius kitty, who has quite an imagination. When you see your cat basking near a window, not quite asleep and not quite awake, don't interrupt her. Though the Aquarius cat is highly social, she is this way because her inner life is so rich that she feels she has much to share. Therefore, if you cut short her dreaming time, she will become irritable and resentful and much less friendly.

Your active Aquarius is often hungry and prefers that you leave food out all the time instead of sticking to scheduled feedings. The Aquarius cat is a snacker and will be very interested in your people-food snacks, too. However, if you offer her your tasty treats too readily, your Aquarius cat will develop a begging problem. You may never eat another meal in peace!

If you have a multiple pet household, Aquarius, being an equal opportunity pet, will never cease to surprise you with how she interacts with the other creatures. This kitty is liberal and extremely open-minded about interspecies friendships. Cats and dogs can get along—if the cat is an Aquarius—but even more remarkably, I've seen Aquarius cats who also get along with rats and snakes!

Aquarius Pawcast

Symbol:
Water Bearer,
a giver of life

Ruling planet:
Uranus, the planet of surprises
and of the unpredictable

Key personality trait:

If the Aquarius cat had a slogan, it would be: "It's All Good."

Would like more:
Cheerfulness. The Aquarius cat
would like it if you were always
in a good mood, walking
around the house while singing
or whistling. This cat loves it
when your friends come over

Cat idol:
cheetah; the
world's fastest
land animal

and wants to make sure that the social schedule is full
of varied and interesting activities. Your Aquarius cat
would also like you to spend more time without the
television on so that she can quietly think.

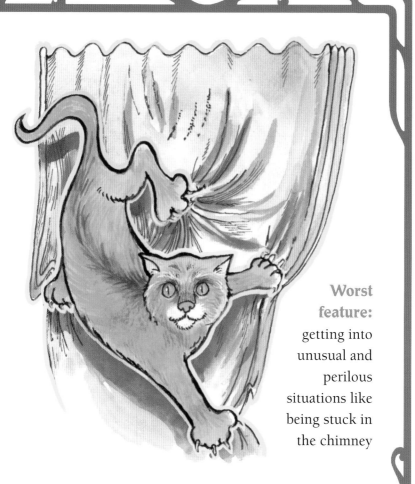

Worst feature: getting into unusual and perilous situations like being stuck in the chimney

Favorite entertainment:

Sports. Live sports are best, but any will do.

Dating style: Zany. Pairing up with her loved ones and knocking things over in the garage might be a great Aquarius date idea, but then, so might getting stuck in a tree. A cat courageous enough to follow this Aquarius into the misadventure du jour is the mate for her. She has many friends and has a difficult time describing the difference between friendship and love. The Aquarius cat is good at keeping things casual—don't bother planning a cat wedding, as she despises such ideas!

Favorite sport: wrestling with other household pets

Pet peeves:

the sound of the vacuum cleaner, the smell of fingernail polish, and when the cops come to break up the party

Best feature: light on her feet

Favorite food:

milk products, like cheese and butter

Favorite thing about owner: your ability to hold up your end of the conversation, your willingness to give a little of your tuna sandwich to a good cause (the hungry cat), and the way you brush her fur

Dreams and fantasies: The Aquarius cat dreams of being an inventor, creating the perfect cat toy or mousetrap. Another favorite fantasy for the Aquarius kitty includes charitable work,

Favorite activity with owner: socializing

like helping creatures on the endangered species list and providing fresh meat for motherless kittens. In all of this cat's fantasies, her human friends are beside her, helping to spread more goodness in the world.

Mantra:

"There's always a better way to get kitty treats, and I will figure out what it is."

The Pisces Cat

T he Pisces cat is a guru and a muse. He has made it his prime purpose in life to become spiritually enlightened, and you, as his owner and friend, play an important role in that quest. By being your imperfect and lovable human self, you provide your cat with lessons in patience that bring him closer to his goal. The spiritual connection that the Pisces cat makes with you enables communication to be simple and precise. At times, you may even wonder if you've met in another time dimension. Your Pisces cat doesn't require that you believe as he does, but he does desire your unconditional love and your non-judgmental ear. A Pisces has much to teach you about how to love and, at times, you'll wonder whether you are taking care of him, or if he is taking care of you.

Though it's wonderful that your Pisces cat is sensitive to your feelings, it's perhaps not quite as wonderful that he is sensitive to environmental changes—temperature, humidity, noise level, new scents, or new people. This touchy cat needs time to warm up to situations. Be prepared to experience his strong resistance to change unless he's absolutely sure that it's for the best. He doesn't even mind the same food week after week; in fact, filling his dish with food that he's not used to will upset his stomach.

The Pisces cat's odd behavior can be a source of wonder and amusement, but it will surely make you see him as a distinct character. For instance, I know one Pisces cat who loathes closed doors and another who only wants to drink from the running tap in the bathroom sink. Try to let your Pisces show you how best to cater to his special needs. This cat knows what is best for him and will let you know his specific needs if you take the time to observe and listen to him. This cat loves to hear you laugh and often joins in, in the silent way that cats do.

A Pisces cat is the perfect companion for senior citizens. Being at the end of the zodiac, this cat has lived many more than nine lives and not only can he appreciate the experience of elders, but he prefers it. Children make this kitty feel a little on edge, as he feels responsible for teaching them respect and manners.

Pisces Pawcast

Symbol:
Fish, riding
the currents

Ruling planet:
Neptune, the planet of dreams
and illusions

Key personality trait:

Unlike so many other cats, the Pisces
cat doesn't take it all too seriously.

Would like more:
Sacred rituals. The Pisces
cat not only needs to feel
secure, but he also likes
to feel as though the
day-to-day things you do
are meaningful. Rituals help
lend the proper solemnity that he enjoys. Putting your
Pisces' water in a special dish and ceremoniously
presenting it at the exact time the clock strikes a
certain hour will make him feel loved.

Cat idol:
Saber-toothed
tiger, an extinct
predator

Dreams and fantasies: The Pisces cat dreams of living in a church, monastery, or temple where he lives a devout life of service and enjoys the camaraderie of fellow truth seekers. The Pisces cat also fantasizes about being a guru in India and teaching humans and other animals through example how to achieve a Zen state of being.

Dating style: Picky. The Pisces cat is fickle and needs a mate who can flow with his ever-changing moods. Such a mate is hard to find; when Pisces meets his dream cat, he will never let go. He prefers to be the leader in the relationship and would like it if the other cat didn't eat before him, and that his mate waited to see where he naps before deciding on a resting place. This is not because the Pisces cat is selfish, but because he is an old soul who has earned the right to be taken care of by his cat friends.

Best feature:
paws

Worst feature:
drooling

Favorite entertainment:

watching Bible study meetings and listening to sacred music, especially anything with the pan flute

Favorite food:
whitefish

Favorite activity with owner:

praying, meditating, and singing

Pet peeves: too many people gathered in one place, the sound of an airplane flying overhead or a passing train, and microwave-cooked food

Mantra:

"If I can believe it, I can do it."

Favorite sport:
fishing

Favorite thing about owner:
your reverence, that you take the time to consider what your place in the universe is, and the way your clothes feel and smell

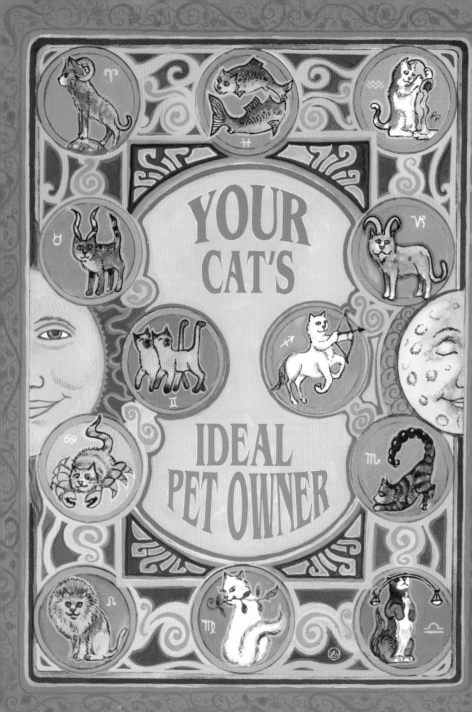

Conclusion

Now that you understand more about your cat by her stars, you can feel more like an ideal guardian who is at ease with your pet's astral characteristics. A clearer understanding of your cat's sign will enable you to tolerate your new pet's shortcomings. Certainly, you can bet your cat will sense your newly discovered love and acceptance. Cats, for the most part, seem indifferent to human activities that do not revolve around their needs and wants. They all but roll their eyes at the owners who expect their cats to do things for them. Aside from the superiority complex, cats are actually more accepting—and even admiring—of humans than appearances suggest. Still, they have their preferences, as detailed below.

Aries. The Aries cat wants an owner with passion, someone who knows what she wants in life. Even though the Aries cat probably won't be able to relate to her owner's goals, she will appreciate the energy that an owner releases. The Aries cat also would appreciate her owner who doesn't mind getting scratched up a bit when playtime gets a little rough.

Taurus. The Taurus cat would prefer an owner who is sensual, someone who makes an effort to create a home atmosphere that engages all of the senses in new and tantalizing ways. For example, he appreciates someone who understands that the same food flavor every day is boring and who cares about the thread count of bed sheets.

Gemini. Ideally, the Gemini cat would have an owner who is spontaneous, someone who keeps a fast pace, a day full of surprises, isn't afraid of interruptions, and enjoys interesting twists. Since Gemini cats like meeting new people and other animals, she likes an owner who welcomes life through the front door. In addition, the Gemini cat likes an owner who reads and shares insights.

Cancer. The Cancer cat would love an owner who is a homebody. The owner values time at home, makes an effort to be in front of the fire on cold nights, sipping a hot drink and not saying a lot. The Cancer cat appreciates a mellow owner, one who doesn't let the outside world have too much of an effect on her inner world.

Leo. The Leo cat wants an owner who is a leader, someone who runs a prestigious household and feels in control. Not every cat can live with the Queen of England, Puff Daddy, or Warren Buffet, but the Leo cat wants to live with someone who at least aspires to be larger than life. The Leo cat always thinks big, so petty owners depress her.

Virgo. The Virgo cat would ideally have a librarian for an owner. He wants someone who enjoys peace and quiet as much as he does; he will adore someone who has read the classics. The other value he holds dearly is structure, so an owner who is on time with food and meticulous about water (purified is appreciated) will enjoy the Virgo kitty's affectionate thanks.

Libra. The Libra cat loves an owner with style, flair, and personality, someone who wears a distinctive cologne or perfume, who likes art, and who drinks coffee in the morning while reading the newspaper. (Or, even better, someone who loves reading a glossy magazine with vivid, glamorous pictures.) The Libra kitty also wants a loyal owner who'll put her first.

Scorpio. The Scorpio cat wants an owner who has sharp instincts, who makes decisions promptly, and who stands by his decisions. Upon choosing a cat to live with, an owner would immediately identify the Scorpio kitty as the perfect choice when he first lays eyes on this sleek, sophisticated feline. The Scorpio cat would prefer not living with children, unless they are very special, savvy children.

Sagittarius. The Sagittarius cat prefers an owner with an independent spirit, someone who understands the concept of freedom, wide-open spaces, and the need to roam. The Sagittarius cat also prefers not to live with a prudish person, as she is not bashful about expressing her sexuality.

Capricorn. The Capricorn cat would like a career-oriented owner, someone who understands the value of hard work because he likes to come to the office once in a while and meet his owner's colleagues. This cat has a career of his own, too, (bird-watcher, mouser, home interior expert) and wants someone who appreciates and respects his important role in the household.

Aquarius. The Aquarius cat likes a zany owner, someone who is not afraid to show eccentricity, and who finds delight in anything weird. The Aquarius cat also likes an owner who throws parties because she likes to maintain a large social network, including humans and different kinds of beasts. An owner who is not too rigid with household rules is best, since the Aquarius cat likes to break the rules just for fun.

Pisces. The Pisces cat wants an understanding owner, someone who appreciates his complex makeup and doesn't take offense or become frustrated with his ever-changing needs—"I want to be petted… no, I don't. I want food…no, not that food!" Since the Pisces kitty gives so much affection and, in a way, spiritual guidance to his human companion, he wants someone who will put up with the occasional slip of bad behavior that he's prone to.

Tuning in to your cat's astrological needs to become an ideal pet owner will create a happier living situation, a greater appreciation of your pet, and a better future. So, put into practice what you have learned about your kitty and give her all the love she deserves.